You

Your diary

Your Best moments

You're the greatest companion!

You're the greatest companion.

Dear diary...

DATE ___________

Dear diary...

Dear diary...

DATE ________________

Dear diary...

DATE ______________

Dear diary...

DATE ______________________

Dear diary...
DATE

Dear diary...
DATE

Dear diary...

DATE _______________

Dear diary...

DATE

Dear diary...

DATE _______________

Dear diary...

DATE ______________

Dear diary...
DATE

Dear diary...

DATE ___________

Dear diary...

DATE ______________

Dear diary...

DATE ____________________

Dear diary...

DATE ___________

Dear diary...

DATE ________________

Dear diary...
DATE

Dear diary...

Dear diary...

DATE _______________

Dear diary...
DATE

Dear diary...

DATE _______________

Dear diary...
DATE

Dear diary...

DATE ________________________

Dear diary...

Dear diary...

DATE ______________

Dear diary...

Dear diary...

DATE ______________

Dear diary...

DATE ____________

Dear diary...
DATE

Dear diary...
DATE

Dear diary...

DATE ______________

Dear diary...

DATE __________________

Dear diary...

DATE ______________

Dear diary...

DATE ______________

Dear diary...

DATE

Dear diary...

DATE ___________

Dear diary...

<u>DATE</u>

Dear diary...

DATE ____________

Dear diary...

DATE ___________

Dear diary...

DATE _______________

Dear diary...

DATE ___________

Dear diary...

DATE ___________

Dear diary...

Dear diary...

DATE ______________

Dear diary...

DATE _______________

Dear diary...

Dear diary...
DATE

Dear diary...

Dear diary...

DATE ___________

Dear diary...

DATE ___________

Dear diary...

DATE ______________

Dear diary...

Dear diary...

DATE

Dear diary...
DATE

Dear diary...
DATE

Dear diary...

DATE ___________

Dear diary...

DATE _______________

Dear diary...

Dear diary...

DATE

Dear diary...

DATE

Dear diary...

<u>DATE</u>

Dear diary...

DATE ______________

Dear diary...

DATE ______________

Dear diary...

DATE

Dear diary...
DATE

Dear diary...

DATE ___________

Dear diary...

DATE ___________

Dear diary...
DATE

Dear diary...

DATE ___________

Dear diary...

DATE ___________

Dear diary...
DATE

Dear diary...

DATE ______________

Dear diary...

DATE ___________________

Dear diary...

DATE

Dear diary...

DATE ___________

Dear diary...

DATE ______________

Dear diary...

DATE ___________

Dear diary...
DATE

Dear diary...

DATE ______________

Dear diary...

DATE ______________________

Dear diary...

DATE

Dear diary...

DATE _______________

Dear diary...
DATE

Dear diary...

DATE ______________

Dear diary...

DATE

Dear diary...
DATE

Dear diary...

DATE ____________

Dear diary...

DATE

Dear diary...
DATE

Dear diary...

Dear diary...

DATE ___________

Dear diary...

DATE

Dear diary...

DATE ___________

Dear diary...

DATE ______________

Your Best moments

You're the greatest companion.!

You're the greatest companion.